AF064146

To those who did what was needed to put the world back to right, thank you.

Acknowledgments

I would like to acknowledge those who have kept our world moving forward and safe in the light of adversity.

CONTENTS

Preface	6
Introduction	7
Lisboa Tarot Majors	9
Lisboa Tarot Minors	45
Suit of Wands	46
Suit of Swords	64
Suit of Cups	83
Suit of Pentacles	101
Spreads	120
Conclusion	127
About Beth Seilonen	128

Preface

The *Lisboa Tarot* was inspired predominantly by a summer visit to the city of Lisbon, Portugal. I spent my days walking throughout the city, photographing the statues and scenery. As time went on, I began to notice correlations to the Tarot held innately within the images. It was as if the Tarot was living throughout the city.

Soon, I was seeing the city through a new perspective, with a connection that was unexpected. A flood of mental impressions of the cards began to flow through my consciousness, an amalgamation of the historical past with the present. Lessons that needed to be told and remembered to help guide us in our present.

While there, I was met with signs and people saying, "Lisboa," the Portuguese word for Lisbon. It seemed appropriate to title the deck, inspired so much from an incredible city, by the name it is known within that country.

The people that are showcased in the cards are statues found throughout the city. As I observed each one, they carried an energy that left me with the impression of who they may have been when living, and that they had advice to share that may help us as we move through our own lives.

I hope that you will enjoy this stroll through this historic city and that the echoes of the past help guide you to a successful future.

Introduction

As I walked through the streets of various cities in Europe, the statues that honored the brave souls and leaders of the past stared down upon me. Raising my eyes to meet those of the past, I wondered what if those souls had known at the time that they were to have a memorial in their honor; what would they have said? What would they have to say about the world as it is now? What advice would they give to help us improve?

There grew a desire within me to bring the insights and knowledge of those who stood memorialized throughout the city of Lisbon to life in the Tarot. Their experiences of hardship, joy, and passion carved upon their faces told of how they lived to their principles even in the face of adversity. Their eyes told of their dedication to pursue their vision throughout their lives.

It struck me that as I give of myself to the betterment of my community and beyond, regardless of how minor it may seem, the importance of being a consistent and intentional model of improvement and inspiration would continue well into the future beyond my lifetime. The souls that were immortalized in stone were the foundations of the vision and culture that made the city of Lisbon what it is today. Their intentions and love were not forgotten.

It is with hope that this deck will help clarify and develop one's vision and assist in understanding the challenges that await. Each moment brings a life lesson and a new layer of wisdom to inspire life to be better than it was the day before.

0: The Fool

Heedless of reality as he casts his eyes firmly to the horizon of opportunity and potential, The Fool walks with ill-advised determination toward his dream. At the back of his mind, he hears his loyal friend barking in a dire effort to bring him back to awareness of his current surroundings, but to no avail.

It is with excitement that we all want to jump into a fresh and new adventure. However, when we have not considered all the facets and implications of what these changes will bring, there is potential failure waiting just one more step away.

Reverse:

As you are visited by this energy, it advises that you really do need to take roughly three, five, or, better yet, ten steps back and sit down. Get well away from the full commitment edge and give yourself a pause to consider the ramifications of what is going on around you. It has been easy to get caught up in the excitement of the moment and to be ready to jump in, but chances are, not everything has been thoroughly explained to you. Best to ask a few more questions before moving forward.

About the Image:
The figure in this card was inspired by the collection of pediment statues located at the Assembly of the Republic, Lisbon.

I: The Magician

The Magician stands ready to advise and teach the visitor to his realm the ways in which each of his tools brings about the magic in one's life. Each time he returns, an opportunity to learn a new aspect emerges. Should he see that some lessons have yet to be completely dealt with, he may repeat them from time to time.

The Magician has well learned his craft and has much to offer anyone who is willing to put in the work. It will always come down to being intentional in your actions and focusing on following through with the necessary steps to make it happen.

When this card comes along, leave The Magician sitting out and shuffle the remaining cards in the deck. As you are shuffling, ask, "What lesson am I to learn?"

Draw a card from the deck in whatever method you desire. Give yourself a moment as you consider the action taking place on the card. What is the meaning or overarching intention of this card?

Once you have the action/intention in your mind, add it to the following statement: "I am to learn how to . . ." Write it down. Consider how this message can help you grow and bring resolution to the situation you find yourself in.

Reverse:
Your reputation precedes you as people are seeking you in order to learn your craft and methodologies of approach to your specialty. Your work appears to come together as if by magic from the outside, and there are those who are eager to understand and embrace your skills.

About the Image:
This card was inspired by the welcoming statue to the left, just inside the narthex of the Basilica da Estrela, Lisbon.

II: The High Priestess

The High Priestess sits upon her altar in quiet connection to the Divine. Her advice and insight are directly related to what she has been told about the situation. She knows the downfalls of insinuating or projecting her own expectations onto anyone. With the Torah in hand to guide, she defaults to the written word for direction as needed.

The High Priestess energy requires one to be honest when seeking her counsel, since she advises only on what she knows. To expect her to make inferences by the partial truths you speak is folly, and the advice will be without meaningful subsistence. The information that you receive back will be reflective of what you are willing to be open about for discussion.

Reverse:

You find yourself in the seat of The High Priestess for others. Be aware that it is difficult for some to be holistically honest about their circumstances, be it embarrassing, uncomfortable, and possibly traumatic; give compassion and respond only to what they have shared with you. If the information is too sparse, be honest and let them know that due to the lack of detail, it is not wise for you to give advice. When working with others, communication should not be a guessing game.

About the Image:
This card was inspired by one of the statues located at the top of the stairs at the Assembly of the Republic, locally referred to as Parlamento (Parliament).

III: The Empress

The Empress is caught in a tender moment of sharing traditions that have been handed down through the generations. She leads through action with her expectations and reverence to customs that she abides. By nurturing the well-being of those around her and herself, she sets the example of what it means to invest in the well-being of others.

You are seen as a compassionate leader. The engaging and supportive energy that you give out to the world works like a magnet to draw people back toward you. Those who come into your inner circle want to support your goals and desires as you support theirs. It is a continual supportive dynamic and well worth every effort to maintain.

Reverse:

You have poised grace, standards, and boundaries. Sadly, there are those who are simply ignorant to anything past their desires and wants. They are attracted to your giving nature and are there only to have their ego stroked. Their selfishness does not warrant your compassion or help in any way.

About the Image:

One of my favorite places in Lisbon, this statue sits in a park beside the Mercado da Ribeira. The Mercado da Ribeira houses vendor stalls with organic, locally grown vegetables, fish, and meat on one side, while the other has a space called Time Out Market, a selection of roughly twenty top restaurants from the city that enables you to have a taste of Portugal in one stop.

IV: The Emperor

The Emperor stands in a commanding pose. A force that leaves nothing in his charge to be questioned. He has a purpose for all, and all would do well to abide by his drive. He honors and recalls the past and what it takes to be a leader at any costs.

As energy of The Emperor enters your life, be prepared. They are going to know exactly what they want, when they want it, and will accept nothing less. This can come off as demanding and impassioned by how their actions have little regard for others. There is simply very little tolerance for anyone who is not going to pull their weight and stands in the way of what they desire. If you are this energy, then may all those who are dead weight have the sense to kindly stand aside before you dismiss them from your presence. The ones who remain will do well to do what is requested as promptly as possible and work to your schedule.

Reverse:

There are walls all around that are holding you to the demands of everyone else around you. Be it career, family, obligations, or more, all insist that they are the most important thing that you must focus your energy on. You will need to muster the energy to set boundaries and priorities on what is most important and what is most reasonable to be addressed in the time it is being asked, then be sure to voice your priorities and what you are able to do to avoid exhaustion or breakdown.

About the Image:

This card was inspired by a statue of Francesco de Sá de Meneses. During the Age of Discoveries, he was one of the noted poets of his time. The intense regard the artist captured caught my attention and was one of the first cards created in this deck.

V: The Hierophant

The Hierophant is the keeper of traditions and beliefs, a teacher of the old ways, and a spiritual guide. Each of beliefs and traditions that are taught is a part of the glue that holds members of the community together. Sanctuary can be found through the open spaces and into the quiet dark alleyways, where one least expects.

The Hierophant enters your life when you need help to guide you to understanding your spiritual path and to better understand that of others. They are here to teach you the traditions and beliefs that have connected communities for generations and what they will continue to do in the many years to come.

Be an active participant when they are advising, since the knowledge and insight they have in conjunction with their experience will help you make the best decision in regard to understanding the best spiritual path for you.

Reverse:

What you feel in your heart as your spiritual purpose is not matching up to what you are seeing being done by others who claim to be of the same faith. There are those who seek to misuse the core foundations of the beliefs and skew them in order to fit the view they want. Be aware of those who wish to misinterpret the traditions and expectations for their own gains.

About the Image:

This card was inspired by two different photos. I found the buildings as I was walking along the back alleyways and came across what looked to be an old church tucked away. The second photo of the statue that is at the top of the entry to the church is Christo Rei, which sits across the bay from Lisbon, watching over the city.

VI: The Lovers

Brought together by their connection and commitment to each other, The Lovers know through the moments of the past and the ones yet to come that each has the power to grow or the power to break their connection. It will take an act of intention with both of the parties to ensure that they grow and support each other.

The Lovers encompass all sorts of love that we have toward others in our world. It is these various nuances of what love is and what it can be that enable us to love people in a wide variety of manners:

friend love, romantic love, platonic love, and so on. Each of these needs to be supported and nurtured if they are to continue to grow and foster in our lives. Those who truly are in this world to be with you are going to ensure that they are reciprocal in their efforts in this relationship, showing that you are loved just as you are.

Reverse:

What started out as mutual growth in love and connection has shifted into being one sided. The love that was once shared has changed into something else, and now it is time to discuss what has caused this breakdown. If this feels like it is past the point of mending, then for the sake of love for yourself and them, support the separation and go with goodwill to find what new love the next chapter of your life may bring.

About the Image:

This card was inspired by the gazebo at the Jardim da Estrela, which sits across the street from the Basilica da Estrela. During the summer months, there are outdoor Latin dance nights in which locals simply show up and dance at the gazebo.

VII: The Chariot

A warrior returns from a war that he did not cause, nor was he able to resolve. He stood for the ethics and beliefs of his countrymen. He fought by their side and moved through the ranks to lead them to victory until the time came to return home as a hero. Looking just outside the city gates, he reflects upon the effects of his actions, the loss of lives at his hands, the trauma. His eyes never quite being of the present as the scars endured would be carried a lifetime in his mind. It was upon his shoulders to ensure that the truth, both the positive and negative, is told in complete transparency.

You have made it through your challenges, learned, and grown into being a highly skilled asset. The strategies you have developed ensure that you are in the best position to take advantage of opportunities as they emerge. Your experiences give you a particular perspective in seeing things within the situation that are nonsensical and are red-flag warnings. Heed them.

Reverse:

Others have approached you to ask for assistance, and by your nature you are more than happy to help anyone in need. However, they have been a bit lackadaisical in their reasons for why they need your help. Before you lose yourself to a situation that may embitter you to those you love, take a moment to sit and have an honest discussion. If they refuse to open up, then it is advisable to pull back your assistance.

About the Image:

The inspiration for this card was found at the monument for King José I.

VIII: Strength

Dignity and composure to walk through any moment in time are the hallmark of this card. Rising above the masses to see clearly to the goal gives one the foresight to know what strategies to take for success. Knowing what is worth the fight and what is best left to its demise, then to follow through, is its own strength.

This card signifies that first, you know who you are; second, you know exactly what you want; and finally, you are willing to do what is necessary to work toward your goal. The necessary work may involve having to stand your ground and fight for your cause. You attend to this in a calm manner, since there is no reason to get angry. To allow for anger to set in will only cause explosive miscalculations in the goals that you have given yourself.

Reverse:

You are not at war with yourself, but at the mechanics that are trying to keep you from your goal. Keep in mind whom you are truly at battle with, and know that they will try to twist the moment to turn it back on you. It is knowing when to fight and when to let go that is the sign of strength in this moment.

About the Image:

The main figure in this card is located at the Dom Pedro IV Square, looking toward the Tagus River, and creates a straight path to the figure found in the Chariot card.

IX: The Hermit

The Hermit desires to be left in solitude as it allows for contemplation of one's past life lessons and to have an honest reflection with the experience. As he works within this mode, he is also afforded the focus to be upon himself and to disengage from emotional entanglements.

This enables The Hermit to build upon his insights, bring clarity to the wisdom he can offer, and ensure that he is holding himself accountable.

It is this manner of accountability that when approached by others, his responses are measured and reflective in regard to his knowledge. He knows to advise only on what will be of use to others in their personal journey.

The journey to The Hermit does have its emotional perils. The process to step back from the business of everyday to take stock of where you are in life can be challenging, since you know you need this time and you crave solitude, but there are responsibilities that still exist.

Set aside time that will allow you to reflect on your past experiences, what you have gained, and what you may need to learn. By better knowing yourself, you are more equipped to clarify your abilities, boundaries, and needs to those who cross your path.

Reverse:
When others come to seek your counsel, be sure that you stay within your realm of knowledge. Refrain from advising on topics of which you have little to no experience within. You will do a disservice to those who most need the help.

About the Image:
This figure is located at the Jarim Dom Luís beside the Mercado da Ribeira. Viewing him from behind, with the curvature of his back, it felt as though he carried contemplative knowledge that I would do well to listen to.

X: Wheel of Fortune

Two sentinels stand on either side of the Wheel of Fortune. They are charged with the task to keep the Wheel spinning from one direction to the other, sometimes slow, sometimes fast, with very little reprieve in between.

The brief moments of respite barely allow one a moment to catch their breath before things are spinning again. When it does, it has a tendency to bring a dash of wealth, abundance, and prosperity into one's world. Then in a swift flick, it all is off and rolling again. It is a time when anything and everything can and will feel like things are happening concurrently.

As this energy comes careening into your life, it is for the best to keep your eyes soundly on where you ultimately wish to be, and to try to stay in the center. It is within the very center of the Wheel where you have the best chances to avoid getting pulled into a situation that is not of your doing, but that others are more than happy to get you involved.

Reverse:

Should you get pulled into the conundrums of others, be prepared that they may potentially saddle you with more work that takes you away from your own personal goals and work objectives.

About the Image:

This card was inspired by the wrought-iron decorative gate found in the narthex (front entry) of the Basilica da Estrela.

XI: Justice

Holding the sword of truth, Justice sits ready to cut through to the truth of the situation. In her hand rests the code of law, by which the lands have agreed to abide by. It is through her that the laws are interpreted and administered to the populous. She holds herself and all others to that standard that is set forth.

The energy of Justice signifies that you need to listen to all sides and listen closely for the facts that are woven into the stories being told. People are going to try to sway the verdict by establishing an emotional connection with you and others to feel their anguish and frustration; a form of emotional manipulation in order to discount the opposing voice. Expect that as you are able to pick up on the facts, this emotional game will no longer work on you.

You are confident in moving forward in the direction that is fair and just as you ensure that all sides will be heard, the outcome will be determined by the evidence, and a fair verdict will be rendered.

Reverse:

You find yourself pleading your case before Justice. Recalling the past without the backup provided by evidence or documentation will be seen as subjective. To help in presenting a clear and unbiased chain of events, locate documents and written correspondence. This proof helps establish a pattern of behavior that will assist in rendering a fair verdict for all.

About the Image:

This card was inspired by the central figure found in the pediment of the Assembly of the Republic, the Parliament.

XII: The Hanged Man

The Hanged Man is caught in a situation he did not create, nor did he seek it out with intention. Suspended, unable to do anything to change his current predicament, he begrudgingly accepts his fate. He has been made to step back from the pace of the world and has to wait until the time comes to be released from the bonds that hold him. He is not in charge of anything at this moment; it is a time of feeling stuck.

As this card appears in a reading, it signifies that the particular situation needs to have a pause given for the time being. There is no rush to resolve or get to the finish line, since there may be other components and nuances that need to be addressed by others first. For the time being, your role has met stagnation. Take this moment and enjoy the short pause, since once the bonds break, you'll be off and running again.

Reverse:

From nothing to something, be prepared for that bump back into reality and projects. You may not have been kept fully aware of the recent developments. This may take a bit to get brought up to speed and find your momentum once again.

About the Image:

This card was inspired by one of the back alleyways in a quiet part of Lisbon that has a series of arches with the nameplate "José Antonio Pereira, April 1805" hung directly under one of the main arches. The region was once the old waterfront, which has since been filled in. I was left with the feeling that this part of town had been frozen in time and was waiting.

XIII: Death

Fear of ending, of closure, sent the man to attempt to cheat fate and undermine Death by stealing his steed to race away into the night. Hoping that upon Death's stallion, he could outrun the inevitable. The bolts of lightning from the heavens halted any notion of changing the future as he was thrown to the ground; the consequence of attempting to change things that are major moments can backlash in ways that are much worse than just facing the inevitable.

Death reminds us of the cycles of life. There are points of closure and openings that we must move through like a personal metamorphosis. Running away from the situation will not prevent change. Be it leaving home, a job, or a relationship, or saying goodbye to a beloved pet or a beloved family and friend, these are points in life that we do need to face, allow ourselves time to grieve, and heal.

The other side of the cycle is the emergence of new things in your life, which is also a form of change. The birth of new ideas, careers, love, a fur baby needing a forever home, possibly welcoming a new child to your family, and so on—these changes also pose their own challenges and stress.

Reverse:

Running away from change is not going to stop it from happening. These shifts need not be met with fear or plotting how to circumvent Death. As hard as it is to have unwanted change happen in your life, a necessary moment in the process of moving forward is to say goodbye.

About the Image:

This card was inspired by a relief carved above the main doorway into St. Paul's Church.

XIV: Temperance

Temperance is the epitome of patience. Knowing herself to be both measured and balanced, she brings about a confidence that emanates from her soul and causes a physiological shift of energy among those she interacts with. She is a calming force that simply puts those at ease, since the flow of energy from one container to the next and back is eternal.

When this energy comes forward, it indicates that you need to take some additional personal time to better know yourself. Use those mental health days, go to the yoga class, meditate, dance, sing, and more. Do whatever is necessary to bring yourself back to inner balance. Then as you approach a situation, keep that self-awareness, that confidence, as you enter into the real world again.

Reverse:

The feelings of being unbalanced, disoriented, and thoroughly discombobulated are apt words to describe how it feels in this moment. You are unsure precisely how you are going to get yourself back to the right way up, and you certainly do not feel that you are at the top of your game to be in control. Instead, others are running the show, and you may find yourself being a participant versus the leader.

About the Image:

The inspiration for this card was found at the base of the Monumento dos Restauradores. I tucked in the wings and pulled the arms down to assist in conveying the energy needed for the card. The background features the Castelo de S. Jorge, which stands over the city.

XV: The Devil

The Devil lures in souls by playing upon the fears that swim at the back of the minds. He encourages those fears to grow and morph into a mindset that debilitates a soul from functioning and moving forward. This trick of the mind entraps the soul to consider that the only safe place is to stay exactly where they are; to attempt to move from what is tangible is to fall into the abyss.

This card signifies that because of the trials that have happened in our lives, we need some type of foundation that provides safety. However, in this situation, it is a false ideal. This foundation has tethered us to a set of societal expectations where "to have it all" means you stay in your space and do not change. This is extremely limiting and unjust in the manner that we need to grow and foster a more healthful lifestyle.

Reverse:

The chains that have held you to material expectations are loosening and falling away, but are you ready to let go? The fears that have long caused you to stay in a toxic place still work hard to convince you that you will fail, that there is nothing out there for you, and that you will be alone forever. This is how fear works; all of it is untrue unless you give it credence and allow it to manifest. Push it back and away; move forward and into the light.

About the Image:

This card was inspired by the statues that sit at the top of the Arco da Rua Augusta just as one walks from the waterfront and across the Commerce Square.

XVI: The Tower

The Tower is very much a part of our lives and how we grow and develop. In the beginning we start with our foundation, constructing it the best way that we know how. As we grow, we continue to add to the building, modifying it as we go along, as we learn better methods. However, we neglect to go back to those foundations to reinforce our early knowledge with what we know now; we just continue to build it up to be as grand as possible.

Soon, what we began does not match who we are at the top; there is a conflict between what was and what now is. Our early foundation can hold up our new selves for only so long before the cracks of the past grow. And with one moment, a gust of wind, and a lightning bolt collides into our Tower; our foundation cannot hold and down it comes.

Everything that is associated with this building—the house of ideas, relationships, life, love—sits in rubble. It is at this moment that you have a choice. You can rebuild your Tower better than before or decide that this is no longer what you are willing to fight for, and leave. It is your moment and a chance in life now; your strings are gone and you are free to branch out and find a new path and a new Tower.

Reverse:

The Tower may be on the verge of collapse, but you are already in a moment of free fall. Appreciate what was, since it will never be the same again. This is a good thing. There were things that were just not secure or safe in your world, and now you have an opportunity to build it better than before. Be sure that you do.

About the Image:

This card was inspired by the Santa Justa Lift, a prominent landmark that is hard to miss. This cast-iron elevator was built in 1902, and it is still in use. In contrast to the brightly colored buildings, to see something predominately black, it gave off an ominous feeling.

XVII: The Star

The Star has retrieved the vessels from Temperance's hand. What was once held in balance, The Star has moved to allow these meditative waters to flow forward. One pours directly to the ocean waters, catching the currents and allowing things to simply go and work their way back in due time. The second vessel is emptied upon the shores. The water creates channels through the land that will stay for a time as it makes its way, reconnecting to the ocean waters, to be free flowing once again.

There are two paths that help move you toward what you want. If you allow your energy to pour directly into your desired destination, it will come about to mix and blend with those of similar nature, and the support is immense. By allowing your energy to start in a different location, it will naturally find its way to join those who are best to support your dreams by creating a path that you can return to time and again. If you ever need to step back and refill your emotional wells, return and your networks will be there, waiting. And this time, by going back to them, the channels grow, becoming more solid and permanently there in your life.

Reverse:

This is a moment that the Star is telling you to take it all back. This path that you wished to have open in your life is just that: a wish that has no substance. The foundation needed to feel secure in investing your time, emotions, and finances in this venture is simply not there.

About the Image:

This card was inspired by the statue of Antonio Ribeiro, a sixteenth-century poet. The Chiado district of Lisbon has an incredible energy that runs well throughout the nights, and only as the sun is ready to emerge does this section of the city truly sleep.

XVIII: The Moon

Glowing full over the slumbering city, illuminating a central monument, The Moon works to play upon the fears that linger from our past. The bayful howls of wolves cut through the solemn night. Searching the clearing to the abandoned streets and alleyways that turn away from our sights, the shadows closing in around us. Fear that stemmed from earlier times, brimming to the surface, affecting the present and potentially the future.

The Moon brings illumination to that which we have yet to overcome in our past. It shows us what traumas we still carry. Be aware that not all traumas can be cured, but when we are cognizant of what contributes to them emerging and affecting our lives, we can take the necessary action to work toward having the growing fear stop in its place, and leave it in the past.

Reverse:

The conflict that you are intuitively feeling is truly happening. There is more that you are being made aware of, and right now listen to yourself and what your body is telling you. Something is amiss, and you will need to take a breath, ground yourself, and then start asking those hard questions of yourself and others. Is this path truly what you want?

About the Image:

This card was inspired by the main statue at the Dom Pedro IV Square, with the Castelo de Jorge in the distance. It is certainly a confliction of choices at this point in the city, since in every direction you go, there are simply amazing experiences awaiting.

XIX: The Sun

Buoyant and blissfully happy, the children welcome and celebrate The Sun back into their lives. They have worked hard to bring their dreams to fruition and now can take a step back, be youthful once again, and embrace the warmth of success.

Just as the children held their sunflowers in celebration of life, the evidence of the brick in the wall tells of the dedication of those who created each brick, set the foundation wall one at a time, and mortared them into place. This step-by-step action, setting forth your action, your intention one at a time, over time builds into a sound wall that exhibits everything that you have put into this moment. Enjoy and reap the rewards of all your time and investment.

Reverse:

You have put your energy fully into the project, and seeing that it is winding down and coming to a close, there is something bittersweet in the moment. You are happy to see that you have successfully brought everything together, but sad that this component is now over and done.

About the Image:

This card was inspired by two incredible places in Lisbon. The sun design hangs in the apse of the Basilica da Estrela, and the child stands at the Jardim Dom Luís, beside the Mercado da Ribeira.

XX: Judgment

Looking down from the heavens, Judgment pondered the situation before calling the souls to awaken one last time. The acceptance of their past lives meant that they had to completely let go of what was once their everything, and be ready and open to allow for a new life to emerge. The acceptance and transformation terrified many. Some would claim that they were ready but would secretly crave to find their way back to the dysfunctional past as fear would creep into their mind.

You are ready to acknowledge what was and who you were by allowing that person or situation to be let go as you accept that it is no longer relevant in your life. You are ready to transform and welcome a new modality and way of being that will further develop you and your happiness.

Reverse:

You are going to dig in your heels and demand that your life is just fine the way it is. This pause on growth is going to encourage stagnation by choice and is often led by fear. What is it that you fear that is preventing you from being everything you have dreamt?

About the Image:

The inspiration for this card was based on a face with the rays emerging above a doorway of the Igreja de Nossa Senhora da Conceição. The graveyard is a combination of Sanctuary of Christ the King in the distance and headstones seen throughout my travels.

XXI: The World

The World signifies that everything has come full circle. It is now the end of the journey that began so long ago with The Fool as merely a dream in his mind. All the trials and tribulations have contributed to illustrate all the dedication it takes to see one's dreams and goals to fruition. Long-term projects have come to completion in a successful manner.

One of the major contributors for success is to be able to manage time effectively. This skill enables you to establish a healthy relationship between your goals and personal life. This pattern of work-to-living ratio will undoubtedly be an advantageous quality to continue to utilize to ensure that your aspirations and dreams are attainable. Regardless of future long-term projects, investments, personal relationships, and more—provided that you are dutifully working toward what you ultimately want, which includes personal growth—there is very little that you will not be able to achieve.

Reverse:

Your world has literally been turned upside down. Everything that you have been working toward has somehow ended up benefiting another, with them receiving the accolades for a job well done. It will take some time to work through difficult feelings of not being properly recognized for your contributions on this project. However, it will happen. Moving forward, it is advisable to be sure that you document your work.

About the Image:

This card is inspired by one of the statues that stand just above the main entrance of the Basilica da Estela.

Lisboa Tarot

MINORS

Suit of Wands

The suit of Wands carries the creative and passionate spark in a reading. The moments that are associated with Wands are often short bursts of time. It does not persist or last. Be sure to harness this energy as quickly as you can, since it is an effective manner in which to get projects jump-started with great excitement. The darker side to this suit is that one can feel overwhelmed when too much gets handed to them all at once. One may have a harder time advocating boundaries since they want to see the ideas come to fruition, but the responsibility just simply lands upon them to keep it going.

Ace of Wands

As the Ace of Wands appears in a reading, it signifies the emergence of an energetically creative moment that has a tendency to sprout new growth in every direction. Be it in love, career, or personal growth, this card is the beginning inspiration that helps get one charged up to tackle the new idea with gusto and excitement.

This is a short burst of energy with potential to have residual effects in whatever region of our life it touches. After the initial burst, the parts that remain can further inspire us to push this idea into a grander concept. Be sure to write down your ideas as they come, so that you can return during a quieter time to reflect upon the potential each one brings.

Reverse: Your mind has gone quiet. After all the racing from one activity to another, one idea to the next, it comes as a relief to simply have silence and nothing to do. Enjoy the moment.

About the Image: This card was inspired by the largest cypress tree in Lisbon, which can be found at the Garden of Principe Real. When I first arrived in Lisbon, my rideshare driver took the time to point out this particular tree. It is simply incredible in person.

Two of Wands

The Two of Wands indicates a time of creative options versus responsibilities. There is an energy that beckons the sentinel to leave their post, venture through the streets, and go beyond their comfort zone to where adventure awaits. The second wand is securely attached to the side of the building, indicating that there are enough creative opportunities to be had at home; there is no need to leave the safe confines.

This card opens up an age-old debate of should you stay where you are at, knowing what you know, in a place that is of comfort or secure for you emotionally? But to grab the opportunity and explore what is just beyond your vision affords you the growth you have been craving of late. The creative energy wants you to drop everything and just be in the moment, while the latter wants you to remain grounded until a more appropriate time. This is ultimately your decision, and whichever way you decide, it will end up being perfectly fine.

Reverse: You are being let loose into the world. There is an effervescent euphoria that surrounds you, since the responsibilities that have long kept you grounded are gone. Now is the time to move forward and explore the world and begin to live your dreams.

About the Image: This card was inspired by a blue building. Due to it resembling a tower and vantage point, it struck me as the perfect place to contemplate staying safe or moving forward to adventure, just beyond where I could see.

Three of Wands

The Three of Wands suggests that this may be a time to invite those in your field to come together to generate new ideas for improvement. By collaborating to develop new methods and strategies, it helps all parties be more productive and successful, supporting each other and increasing the quality of the service or item. It requires that those who come to the table let go of their egos and bring ideas and a clear mission in mind to improve the situation for all parties.

This application of bringing all the stakeholders together to collectively discuss the issues at hand and then to actively begin to develop ideas that may help improve life for everyone is the focus of this card. Small actions over time will make a big change, but there needs to be that initial moment to have an open dialogue and willingness to discuss and solve the issues.

Reverse: At this time, those stakeholders who have a vested interest are currently still in the realm of taking the options and considering how they benefit from the agreement. They are really interested only in what is your compromise to meet their needs. If you were hoping for a reciprocal event, then you may wish to reschedule for a later date.

About the Image: This card was inspired by a relief I saw on the opera house and from the incredible tile work found throughout the city.

Four of Wands

The Four of Wands welcomes in the moment of joy and celebration in one's life. Be it a union, an anniversary, or the beginning of a new life choice, be sure to embrace the moment. The happiness of the event creates a bank of warm memories to reflect upon with your loved ones in the years to come. Celebrate and celebrate big!

Be sure to share the joy and love that you have in your life with those you hold dearest. Be it family get-togethers, weddings, baby showers, birthdays, promotions within one's career, or any joyful occasion that is important to you, bring together people who have supported you and love you throughout the journey. These are the cherished moments that stay with us through the years and bring light to our darker days.

Reverse: There is a suggestion that people are celebrating anything and everything for the sake of keeping the party going. When this happens, the moments that were at first filled with happiness and cheer are now the norm and no longer hold any kind of specialty. They have become common and have diminished the purpose of celebrating.

About the Image: This card was inspired by the gazebo that sits in the Jardim da Estrela. One can find impromptu dancing there in the evenings, with lots of positive vibes.

Five of Wands

The Five of Wands indicates that there are plenty of personalities ready to pitch that perfect idea to you. They all want to have their creative and passionate voices heard and are more than happy to beat the others out from presenting. Each of them feels that if they could talk just a little louder, be a bit more boastful, they would get chosen.

You are definitely a part of this dynamic. You realize that you are going to have an added edge to your plan to ensure that your idea is heard. Be ready to have a counterargument for why you are the better choice over everyone else, knowing that they are going to be more than willing to take up arms and find weak points in your proposal.

Reverse: You may have a couple of the Wands in hand to give you a slight advantage; however, your competition has situated their Wands so that you and they are caught. The Wand that you chose not to raise in battle has gone largely unnoticed. It is this idea that you have kept quiet about that has the best opportunity of success. Be sure to reveal it at the right moment.

About the Image: This card was inspired by the João de Deus statue located in the Jardim da Estrela.

Six of Wands

The Six of Wands celebrates a victorious return home. The ideas and goals that were at the heart of the endeavors have been most fortuitous and successful. The success is not only for the rider, but for all who have supported them; each of the Wands held by the unseen people behind the horse is just as responsible for this moment as the rider. This moment of pride is warranted by all.

You have made your community proud. They have supported you in your dreams, and to see you return as everything they knew you could be, they are filled with pride to call you one of their own. You have worked hard for this moment, and every accolade is well earned.

Reverse: Someone has been celebrated for their work, when in reality they did not do the work and have taken credit for another's effort. It will come to light in due time that they have committed fraud. The consequences for this will be felt for many years to come in many different components of their lives.

About the Image: This card was inspired by the monument to King José I.

Seven of Wands

The Seven of Wands card recommends that one stands their ground in light of adversity. The ideas that are bouncing around are not going to be supported by others, and many will be happy to undermine in any way the work and positive ideas that have been developing. Usually, this is due to an unwillingness to see how the ideas and changes are going to create a positive shift in the situation. There is also a sense of staying with what they have always done, and a sheer resentment toward any notion of nonconformity.

This is not a time to take things personally. The people who are trying to cast you in a bad light are threatened by your ideas. They see your solutions as a sideways method of telling them that they are no longer relevant to the situation. You know that this is not the case; you are truly looking to find a creative solution that will help everyone. Stand your ground.

Reverse: They are able to push you a little too far, and it sends you toppling from your perch. Once you recover, you may do well to try a different tactic. Instead of taking on everyone at once, move to discuss your ideas in a small group or in a one-to-one situation. Chances are you will have more success.

About the image: This card was inspired by one of the statues found watching over the plaza just outside St. Paul's Church.

Eight of Wands

The Eight of Wands signifies that the difficulties and hurdles faced in getting ideas off the ground have cleared away. Each of the Wands is independent of the others; they do not cross with another Wand. This is an important development since the ideas are sound and whole in themselves.

You can expect to be able to move forward smoothly toward your next goal, and don't be surprised if you really start cruising along at a faster and faster pace. As one idea leads to the next, and to the next, you are able to move deftly between them as needed and will have the freedom to do so.

Reverse: Your ideas, though grounded, are taking longer for you to see them developing properly.

This could be bad timing, since the systems to support your vision may not have all their components in place, and you may need to hold off for a bit longer.

About the Image: This card was inspired by my photo capturing both the 25 de Abril and Sanctuary of Christ the King together and reflecting upon the love of their nation that moved a country from Fascist to democratic.

Nine of Wands

The Nine of Wands tells of the emotional toll it takes on a person who is working tirelessly on their goals and has been undermined time and again by those who do not believe in their goals and dreams. They are exhausted. But in the exhaustion is determination to ensure that their passions and ideas come to fruition regardless of the naysayers.

You are close to success and are in the final moments to see your dreams come to reality. This is one of the harder moments to push through, since you have been working long and hard to get to this point. You hold the final component in your hands in a defensive manner, almost as if a bit fearful over what will happen when you no longer have to be caught in this modality and are able to take a breath.

Reverse: The constant battling has left you feeling that you no longer know what precisely you are fighting. It started out a long time ago with wanting an effective change for the betterment of everyone involved, but of late, it feels that the passion for the ideal is no longer driving you. You are driving yourself out of spite.

About the Image: This card was inspired by a figure found in the pediment of the Assembly of the Republic.

Ten of Wands

The burden of the Ten of Wands rests in that all the responsibility of the Wands falls squarely upon the back of one, and they are overwhelmed. The weight of every idea, passion, and dream creates a dynamic where the one held responsible feels isolated and that only they can accomplish the work: if they fail, then they have failed everyone. They do not wish to complain or ask for help.

You have a lot of pride and want to continue to be strong in light of everything that has happened. Being responsible for everything that has happened also means to be responsible for things yet to come, such as your mental well-being. By working continually to take care of others, by taking some of their burdens and adding them to yours, may seem at first to be an act of love. The reality is that you are allowing them to skip over learning how to manage their own responsibilities. You are adding too much to your already filled plate. Soon it is going to crack. Best to reflect on each of the responsibilities: Are there any that could be resolved easily and in a short amount of time? Take care of those first. Then work back through each of the situations as you can.

Reverse: You have been a blessing for so many for a very long time. They have indeed counted on you to be there to ensure that they would be taken care of in any event. Now is the time that they will need to take ownership of their responsibilities. They created the issue, and they can take care of it. It is not your duty to take care of everything.

About the Image: This card was inspired by a statue of Mary sitting on a donkey on the grounds of the Basilica da Estrela.

Page of Wands

This child has a spitfire personality that will forever be an inspiration for the creative opportunity and optimism. As this energy comes into your life, be prepared; there is very little this child would ever consider impossible. Everything is possible, absolutely achievable, and it should all be started right now without hesitation or delay. Just say yes!

The energy of this card simply calls to be utilized in igniting the latent passions that have been long ignored or dismissed as a folly or dream of a misguided fool. It would be absurd to continue to ignore the calling to give into the dreams that have sat with you for a lifetime. If you were waiting for an invitation to start, this would be it.

Reverse: While jumping full gusto into the dream is not appropriate at this time, it is well worth setting the flame of an idea at the back of your mind. This will afford you time to allow the idea and dream to grow, giving yourself time to explore the potential and plan how you can make it move into fruition in an organized manner.

About the Image: This card was inspired by a statue found at the Jardim Dom Luís.

Knight of Wands

The Knight of Wands indicates that you should go after an idea that has ignited the passion within you. It is well worth seeing where it may lead, all the possibilities, and to enjoy the adventure along the way. To step away from what could be will certainly be a regret over time as you ponder what could have been had you simply followed your passion.

When this energy, or person, enters your life, imagine what your life would be like with your goal already achieved. Take note of how it feels to have this in your life. Now with a clear vision, follow that passion, and regardless of if it all works fluidly or not, at least you were willing to go after your dream.

Reverse: You have reservations about simply charging forward and into the unknown. This pursuit of an ideal is too extreme for you, so while you are happy to set small attainable goals, you are not ready to head off to realms that are not familiar and may have you feeling that you are leaping off a cliff of faith.

About the Image: This card was inspired by the monument of King José I, looking to the west toward 25 de Abril and the Belem, a strategic post to protect the city from times long past.

Queen of Wands

The Queen of Wands is an independently creative force that has the power to charm any room she walks into. Her energy simply fires up those she comes into contact with, and they are quick to want to take on and complete any task that she sets forth. She is utterly charming, with a fiery spirit, and many would do wise not to upset her, since she does have a temper about her that can shift quickly before you have a chance to pull back your words.

As you have this energy, or this person enters your life, expect that you are going to be able to charm just about anyone with your gracious wisdom and inspiring vibration, which simply draws people to you. It is this draw that will enable you to find just the right people to pull together your plan. With your skills of managing people and delegating, it will appear seamless as everything just falls into place.

Reverse: You are quick witted, and others are barely able to stay one step ahead of you since you have a sharp eye and ear to be able to determine who is not going to be the team supporter that you need. You are quick and dismissive to those whose energy does not match your own; they are simply a drain upon you.

About the Image: This Queen card was inspired by the stone wall and ruins found from an old lookout point at the Jardim da Estrela, and a statue in one of the small plazas located throughout the city.

King of Wands

The King of Wands has a charismatic personality, and, like the Queen, people are drawn to follow him to see his ideas brought to fruition. He is able to establish a healthy work-to-life balance because he is able to let go of micromanaging his day-to-day life, since he has people for that. He simply states an idea and will manage the right people to do the job successfully.

When this energy emerges in your life, know that you have the experience to put together the right team of people to help you bring your idea to fruition without having to get down and working on the more menial tasks that can simply be hired out. The confidence that you radiate draws more people who want to work with you on bringing all you dream to success.

Reverse: You have a strong and bold personality that can make others uncomfortable in speaking their concerns to you. Pull back a bit and listen to what they are saying, since their words may have an observation or idea that can make your project that much better.

About the Image: This card was inspired by one of the lead poets from the sixteenth century who are honored at the Praça Luís de Camões.

Suit of Swords

The suit of Swords brings clarity in intellectual pursuits and direct communications. This suit is known for cutting directly to the truth. It may seem harsh when people speak from the heart of their concerns, but it provides for transparency and honest discussion of the situation, which will then allow for everyone to move forward. The Swords are also known for being very black and white in personality; whatever the rule book says is precisely what they will do as it applies to their situation.

The Swords are a suit that will turn your words and actions against you through logic. Be sure that you keep your behaviors and statements truthful. They have an innate ability to know the moment a person has lied, and they will not forgive or forget.

Ace of Swords

The Ace of Swords brings new strategies for better and more effective communication. The nature of this card supports the initial actions and conversations needed to occur with clarity for new projects to be embraced. By avoiding any communication breakdowns, new projects are able to move along in quick succession since the expectations are clear and concise.

Your communication has taken on a new level of clarity. When presenting to others, you are able to deftly address the concerns in a quick and forward manner. There has also been a development in the skills of discernment, particularly in regard to what people are alluding toward as they cloud the space by speaking partial truths. You succinctly wield the blade to cut through the confusion and bring everyone back to the point of the conversation.

Reverse: Though you are working hard to bring your ideas to the table, there are past moments of miscommunication that are impeding this from coming together. It is advisable to go back and clear the air so that you and others who are involved can move forward.

About the Image: This card was a nod to the memory of those who took action against fascism by placing the 25 de Abril bridge into the scenery and by following through with their voices for what Portugal needed and what was right for its citizens.

Two of Swords

Blinded to what is there and what is not, the bearer of the Two of Swords keeps them close, ready to use should the moment arise. He is left trapped in his mind, unsure if what he thinks is happening truly is, or if it is simply a trick of his imagination. Reliant upon the communication of others to be able to move through this moment, sadly he is left in the dark, alone in his thoughts.

You find yourself at a stalemate. No one is communicating what is going on in the larger picture, and they have decided to leave you in the dark. There is literally nothing you can do until someone comes along to help you sort out things. Be patient.

Reverse: You are tired of waiting for people to simply be honest with you with the situation. As frustration to what is being withheld grows, you lash out wildly, not knowing, or particularly caring at this point, who gets hurt. The desire to make others have some sense as to how their actions have affected you is overriding your practical side.

About the image: This card was inspired by a statue that sits just outside the Jardim da Estrela in a roundabout titled "Pedro Alvares Cabral Monument."

Three of Swords

Interwoven into the iron filigree heart, the honesty of the conversation has left its mark permanently embedded into the very structure. The Swords were craftily wedged into place intentionally in careful consideration, to ensure that the lesson that came with each would never be forgotten or simply be removed when one tired of them.

This card is about not only how we receive and process honestly, but also how we are truthful with others by having empathy in how our honesty affects others. By being aware of our role, we ensure we are respectful and supportive of growth as parties move forward, regardless of if it is together or apart. These lessons of heartbreak will be carried potentially for a lifetime. Be honest, and be mindful of the marks you leave upon hearts.

Reverse: Sometimes there is absolutely no way of understanding why someone has lashed out as they have, be it in a relationship or work dynamic. It truly is time for you to walk away. There is nothing remaining that is worth continuing to build upon. By allowing the door to close and giving yourself time to grieve and process the moment, you will have a better perspective of the events that lead up to the final moments and be able to pick them out sooner if you see the same behaviors emerging again.

About the Image: I was intrigued by the heart-shaped, wrought-iron decorative element I found one afternoon when in search of delicious pasteis de nata. Much to my sadness and heartbreak, my favorite place had sold out before I got there.

Four of Swords

The Four of Swords signifies that it is necessary to withdraw from the steady barrage of needs, expectations, and conflicts that are constantly being faced. Three of the Swords have been hung upon the wall, each representing an ongoing concern or issue. The fourth has been laid to the ground, and the decision made to simply allow it to dissipate out of awareness, to simply not care about it anymore, allowing the quiet and contemplative time to occur for a much-needed mental health break.

You have pushed yourself tirelessly every day to meet every goal and every situation that has emerged, giving all that you have. Depleted physically and emotionally, it is time to take time for yourself to recoup and recharge. Do so as soon as you can.

Reverse: Time to hand back those Swords and take away some of the responsibilities that you have been charged with. If you need to walk away from projects to keep your sanity, then do it. This will further help you recover and rejuvenate.

About the Image: This card was inspired by one of the figures to the right side of the pediment found at the Assembly of the Republic. His expression conveyed the exhaustion one faces as they strive to put to right the wrong.

Five of Swords

This card captures the moment right after the conflict, when one is left to pick up the pieces. Once they were able to share the responsibility of the Swords, now all the accountability fell to their feet. The other party simply decided to walk away from the situation, letting go of any obligation that remained.

Once the words are out, there is simply no way to pull them back. Be sure to say precisely what you mean. Be ready for others who do not agree to what you want to see changed, or who aren't willing to work with you on your concerns, since they may simply leave. This means that you will now be accountable for everything. Before engaging, be sure that you have a plan to ensure that you are able to handle all the responsibilities that come with this choice.

Reverse: You know that you are not in the wrong, but every time you try to engage to have a resolution occur, it is simply one barrier after another. You have met the point of no return; the toxic nature of the situation is simply not worth your health to continue to fight to stay. There is a relief in being able to simply let go of the Swords and walk away.

About the Image: This card was inspired by the Jardim 9 de Abril, a park that overlooks the bay and 25 de Abril bridge. The figures range from the Praça Luís de Camões to the Basilica da Estrela.

Six of Swords

The conflicts that have continued to go unabated have simply become overwhelming, since it feels as if they are nonstop, coming in wave after wave, threatening to take the soul out to deeper realms. There is barely enough time to get one's feet underneath before the next surge comes. Now is the time to put in the extra effort, pack up, and navigate those treacherous waters in search of calmer, safer harbors.

There is no need to continue to stay in the chaos, since eventually it will take you well beyond your threshold of equilibrium. Be aware that as you work to remove and distance yourself from the constant barrage and conflict, the contention does not simply go away. It is still there, and it is going to follow you regardless of where you go. It is advisable to take the time you need to get your feet back under you and then work through this point by point, addressing the issues in order to truly lay them to rest and keep your harbor calm.

Reverse: Once you have a moment to leave the turmoil of the situation, you are able to see through a new lens truly how minor the issue was. The people at the heart of driving the chaos had you feeling that your only option was to run. Now that you know, you can make the choice to return or remain on a new path.

About the Image: This card was inspired by the marina that sits underneath the 25 de Abril bridge. The bridge commemorates the Carnation Revolution, when the military rose up against a Fascist leader and moved Portugal toward democracy.

Seven of Swords

Dancing with the swords, maneuvering his body and feet in quick time to avoid getting caught by the falling blades. There is a trickery of movements, a repositioning of weight and hand to shift the energy of direction one way to the next without seeming as though anything had been intentional to the onlookers.

Being able to keep the beat, take care of what you can, and sidestep with grace and poise that which you have deemed too much will stun those around you. The confidence in your actions is so smooth and concise that they pay little heed to what you are tossing away and what you are keeping. This is where the cunning and manipulation of the moment happens. By being charming and unassuming, it distracts others enough for you to be able to keep all the best things.

Reverse: May this serve as a warning that someone around you has been putting on a false bravado to distract from their true intentions. They may be working to have the accolades for work shift to them for a promotion. Their smooth actions and words convinced others of their narrative, and they now reap the rewards.

About the Image: This card was inspired by a hand-painted tile piece found on the side of a building, and an evening photo of a street leading to the waterfront.

Eight of Swords

Trapped by what he doesn't know, he finds himself unsure as to how to set himself free. He is unable to clearly see a way to improve his situation, so there he stays, in the constrictive framework of the bonds that hold him ignorant and a prisoner.

It was easy at the beginning to simply ignore the small things. However, those small things continued to accumulate, and now you are stuck with feeling overwhelmed. Take a moment and look to see what you can easily address and take care of by communicating your needs. Help is there; you just need to ask.

Reverse: All the conflicts that have been building up around you are going to be staying for a while, until you are ready to work yourself free of the real issue that is keeping you from moving forward. This is going to take an honest internal dialogue and accountability, but you are able to do so. Once you do, you will be able to clearly see a way to move around the conflicts and to better times.

About the Image: Tucked away across the road from the Assembly of the Republic is one of the many staircases that allow citizens to easily move through the city. Fair warning should one approach these areas without a map: it is very easy to get lost where the cars don't go.

Nine of Swords

Riddled with nightly terrors, they fed upon his fears and plagued him through the night and into his dreams, bending his mind into believing he was dissolving into irrelevance from all he loved in the whole. He sat in a state of shock, unable to wake from the horror, until finally he was gone and into the abyss, only to gasp and awake back into this world.

It is important to remember that the fears that ebb through our minds at night and work into our dreams are baseless. They are simply the far reaches of the mind working to gain prominence and, in this moment, succeeding. Turn on the light and write down the concerns and thoughts. When morning arrives, review, reflect, and possibly discuss with a trusted friend or counselor, since once we address and voice our fears, that is the way we can begin the work to resolve them.

Reverse: Document your concerns that are growing at the back of your mind. Once you have the list, counter each with a positive message or an easy-to-accomplish action that would address the fear. Then, when these thoughts cross your mind, counter it instantly to put it to rest.

About the Image: This card was inspired by one of the iron busts located in the Jardim da Estrela. He struck me as someone who had seen nightmares yet moved forward, facing each and every one in the light of day.

Ten of Swords

The moment came when he realized that all the blame had been placed squarely upon him. He raised his hand to ward off the lies, the doubt that was cast, the misunderstanding, but to no avail. Being made the villain in another's story made him a victim in his own narrative.

There is not much you can do at this time in regard to how others have portrayed you, and you are acting through what they believe. Regardless if true or not, they are past the point of listening to you proclaim your innocence. They have made up their mind and are following through to sever any alliance they once had with you. Take a breath, since once this passes, you will be better off to have them out of your life, because those who are unwilling to sit and communicate their concerns in a reasonable manner may have a host of other dysfunctional behaviors far worse. Count your blessings.

Reverse: You have allowed for the feedback of others to turn into a personal attack where there was none. Feedback that does not agree with your assessment is simply that, just a suggestion, and does not warrant you to simply throw your hands in the air and quit. Stick to what you feel is the best for you, voice it, and carry on.

About the Image: This card was inspired by one of the statues that stood at the Pedro Alvares Cabral Monument, just outside the Jardim da Estrela.

Page of Swords

A youthful child races onto the scene full of new ideas and perspectives, ready to lead the way. They are protective of what they consider their intellectual property and are keen to maintain what they consider important to them. This child has a knack for quick wit and direct communication. They have little time for arguing, since they are very self-assured that they are right before they even begin to talk.

When this energy comes into your life, expect that you are going to be boundless with inspiration that will help not only you but others by allowing for new perspectives to come into conversation. These conversations will bring about a host of new planning to bring the ideas to fruition. Be sure to speak or write down everything that comes to mind during this time. Being of youthful energy, it happens for a short burst of time. Make the most of it!

Reverse: You have found yourself wasting your time in small, meaningless arguments with others who refuse to even consider a new perspective. Try as you will to push what you see so clearly as a positive move, it is simply not worth your continued energy. Seek out others who are willing to invest and support this endeavor.

About the image: This card was inspired by one of the staircases found throughout the city to help citizens move through this hilly area. The child was inspired from the statues found in the Jardim Dom Luís.

Knight of Swords

The Knight of Swords charges into the situation driven for success, so much so that he doesn't always consider the repercussions of his actions, feeling that the ends justify the means. This can come off as a bit abrasive and cold to others. His confidence in his actions does not belay even when it becomes evident that his foundations are not as secure as he has led others to believe.

You need to dive into the project that your heart truly believes is worth the effort, regardless of the repercussions on others. The ideas and planning that you have invested need to have the action added to begin the process to bring it to fruition. Your ability to articulate and inspire through your drive will attract the right people to support you.

Reverse: You may have the ideas and the drive to accomplish a lot, but do you have the necessary foundations and knowledge needed to bring this forward? If you do not, then reach out and locate others who do have the knowledge and are compelled to make this endeavor successful.

About the image: This card was inspired by the statue centerpiece located at the monument of King José I.

Queen of Swords

Clear and decisive, this Queen has little tolerance for the fools of the world. She sees every situation in black and white; there are no allowances for gray. When working with her, one would be wise to be mindful that there is little that she forgets and that she is accomplished in her own brilliance. She has little time for games, can quickly see through the play, and can bring it to a succinct end.

As this energy comes into your life, you carry an expectation that people are going to be honest and straightforward in what they need and want. There is also an expectation that when you speak, people are to follow through promptly with what has been asked. In order to get what you need done, there is simply no time to have to go back and ask again. It will be very hard to simply not cut these people out of your project and your life.

Reverse: You have become intolerant of people who simply are not respecting your boundaries or your expectations. It is time to set them straight and hold them to what you know they are capable of. If they continue to fail, it may be time to set further boundaries and cut back on how involved they are in your life.

About the Image: This card was inspired by the stone wall and ruins found from an old lookout point at the Jardim da Estrela, and a statue in one of the small plazas located throughout the city.

King of Swords

Astute and keen upon his intellectual pursuits, this King enjoys his daily patterns since they add structure to his day. Whereas the Queen will set the structure within her social and work circles, the King is mindful that he can truly control only himself and his own actions. He is driven and, when working with others, certainly does expect them to know fully of his accomplishments and respect his authority in his realms of knowledge.

When this energy comes into your world, it is best to utilize this to focus on what you need to do to be the best in your field of expertise. You already have the foundations and are gaining experience; what more could you do to push toward the next level? Keep on going to be your absolute best in your realm.

Reverse: You have been aware of your consistent investment into yourself and have seen the rewards. But in this moment, you paused to briefly observe your surroundings and have noticed that those around you have remained stagnant. Allow this brief moment to act as a drop in the veil so that you could see honestly past your own walls.

About the Image: This King card was inspired by one of the lead poets from the sixteenth century who are honored at the Praça Luís de Camões. This particular one stands at the very top of the collection.

Suit of Cups

The suit of Cups focuses on emotions and mental well-being. The feelings that we carry into a situation will directly affect our well-being. It is important that as we better understand our emotions, we are then equipped to work with the pros and cons in regard to the impact that situations have on our mental health. This introspection enables us to make a sound choice that puts our needs first, and to decide if it is best to continue to pursue a direction or if it is best to leave.

The Cups also allow for us to approach situations with empathy and compassion, ready to assist and help others through their times of need. As we each move through this suit, we are able to grow toward our better self through continual self-awareness.

Ace of Cups

This is just the beginning. Emotions that have been contained behind the vessel's walls have swelled beyond the barrier and have burst forward. The torrent of emotions flows through one unrelentingly. From extreme happiness and love to sadness and anger, they come in waves, burning and marring the soul for an eternity.

This is the beginning of new experiences that will grow your emotional well-being. You may see deepening connections in your life in regard to career or love, and also a greater sense of love and compassion for the self. It is a reminder that you are indeed vibrantly alive, feeling things deeply and passionately.

Reverse: You have been holding back and suppressing your emotions for a long time. As much as you have withheld, they are finding unhealthful ways to emerge. It may be difficult to share how you feel with those at the heart of the situation, but you will need to before everything becomes too much and it comes forward in utter emotional chaos.

About the Image: This card was inspired by one of the many fountains located throughout the city, seeming to ignite the passions for all things beautiful.

Two of Cups

Two souls affirming a loving and supporting commitment to one another. Each pledging to be loyal, to honor, and to keep sacred their emotional health and wellness to the other. These commitments push for both parties to be present and active in the relationship.

This is a time to take in the vows that you have made to those you love, and to ensure that you are being active in that moment with them. Listen without comment; play and laugh in the moments that you share with each other. Moments can be brief, but when added up across a lifetime, they become the warm memories we cherish.

Reverse: There have been things brewing for a long time that have not been brought to the surface and discussed openly. Will the truth potentially be upsetting and painful? Possibly. However, keeping secret how you are changing or your concerns is doing more harm than good.

About the Image: This card was inspired by one of the pillars with a top decorative motif. Inside the ball that sits at the top, a lion from the Jardim Dom Luís sculpture found its way into the card.

Three of Cups

Being with close friends who know of the paths each other has taken, some extremely difficult, challenging, and dark, with sinister twists. Yet, all have made it out to lighter and joyous times. It is time to celebrate each one's growth toward becoming stronger, more confident, and wiser.

Take that afternoon off with your friends, go on that weekend trip, or hop in the car with your friends to go out for the day. Do the things that bring you back to building and connecting with your friends, celebrating the world and the moment it finds you in. You and they have come so far, and we need to be mindful to continue to hold each other up.

Reverse: The people whom you have been connecting with may have superficial or surface-level feelings for you and may not be all that interested in developing deeper friendships. Be honest in reflecting how you connect with them and how they reciprocate. Do they?

About the Image: This card was inspired by the statues located in the Jardim da Estrela.

Four of Cups

The Four of Cups sits and will wait until just the right one comes along. They are in no rush to simply grab whatever emotional well is right in front of them, but will reflect on precisely what they want in their lives. They accept nothing but what is going to be a perfect emotional match for them.

Reflect on what kind of emotional health you want in your life. Be it quality of food, workplace environment, love, life experiences; this card tells us to pause for that moment and feel out what we really want that will be reflective of our own emotional happiness. Then when the opportunity comes, we will know to simply reach out and grab it.

Reverse: What you have dreamt is just outside your reach. You may be so focused on the emotional entanglements and responsibilities that run riot in your life that to even consider one more is simply too much. Even if that one more thing has been what you have always wanted, you may need to hold and maintain what you already have before you bring additional elements into your life.

About the Image: This card was inspired by the statues that sit at the base of the Monumento dos Restauradores.

Five of Cups

Sitting alone atop the pedestal, he watched as his Cups careened toward the floor. He made no move to stop the process, instead losing himself in the pit of self-wallow as he bemoaned his losses. Regret plagued him as he realized that their downfall was due to his own neglect in paying attention to his actions.

Inadvertently, we are often the cause of our own misery. When preoccupied, we often forget to be present and stay aware of our surroundings and of the people within the space. Emotional mishaps are normal, and there is simply nothing you can do to fix them at this time. However, even within this moment as things go wrong, if you carefully turn around, you will see that there are still good moments and relationships in your life.

Reverse: You are so completely engrossed in watching the Cups fall away that you have forgotten entirely about the other two Cups. It is well within expectation that should you lean over the edge even more to see where the other Cups have fallen, you may end up kicking what you have left off the edge, truly leaving you alone on your pedestal.

About the Image: This card was inspired by a collection of statues carved together; when pulled apart, the singular impact of his body language could be felt.

Six of Cups

The couple stood at the waterfront, watching the tides of time move through the bay. He turned to give her a bouquet. Touched by his gesture, she held her Cup ready to set the flowers in, to help preserve the gift and moment as long as possible. The memory and connection in that moment lasted well into the future.

The Six of Cups is in the realm of gift giving. To give and take through compassion and love; it is these actions that generate a tangible sense of kindredness and empathy.

Through the act of giving and seeing it received in appreciation and joy, it feeds into a well of happiness and euphoria when a simple act means so much to another. We feel that energy as it comes back many times over, which then helps build our emotional well of happiness. When they give back, it simply continues to grow beautifully.

Reverse: You have been giving more and more of yourself of late. It does stand to ask, at what point do you feel you have given too much? Others have simply come to expect you to always say yes and to give whatever you have to their cause, without being reciprocal in any measure.

About the Image: This card was inspired by the statues found at the Basilica da Estrela.

Seven of Cups

He stood on the edge of the pier with hat in hand, waiting and watching. He watched as all his dreams and desires assembled upon a cloud, carried away by the winds to distant lands, and pondered if his dreams would ever come to be. He gave voice to that which he most desired as they sailed away, hoping that his words would carry and the wish would come to fruition.

This is the wish card. Be mindful that not all wishes are granted; however, it does begin with voicing precisely what you want to welcome into your life. Envision it coming to you and how you would feel with this desire manifesting in your life. Keep that feeling and emotion strong in your mind as you put the wish to the winds.

Most wishes will have a better opportunity of coming to fruition if one has done the back work to enable and support the wish to manifest. Watch for the opportunities and remember to say yes.

Reversed: Your dreams and emerging opportunities will remain in the wish realm. There is more work that needs to be done to ensure that when they are granted that you have the best foundation to support their growth in your life.

About the Image: This card was inspired by the 25 de Abril bridge, which received its name from the date in 1974 when the military rose up against the Fascist leader and brought democracy to Portugal. It was a nod to those who stood for dreams and aspirations of all who followed.

Eight of Cups

He gave everything he could emotionally to have the situation improve. Then came the moment when he knew he could not keep putting everything forward with no emotional return. It was time to cut his losses and walk away.

Realizing that all you have done to salvage your relationships and emotional health has been for naught. If the other parties are absolutely resolved not to work through the situation, there is truly nothing that you can do, and now is when you need to walk away to find more-healthful relations.

Reverse: The emotional toll taken on others has been dumped on you time and time again. You can continue to bear witness to being the dumping ground for only so long before you need to walk away and establish boundaries in order to preserve your relationship.

About the Image: This is along the hillside as one is ready to walk down toward the Praça Dom Pedro IV. Along the stairs, there was always a homeless woman begging for change, wanting to leave the life in which she found herself. In the distance, Castelo de São Jorge rises above the landscape.

Nine of Cups

Every moment of growth that has happened is directly due to the intention and work one has put into achieving the goal. It is a time to stop and reflect. What was once a dream is now reality.

Through perseverance and fortitude, you have manifested the narrative that now exists. Within this narrative are characters that have supported your journey and will continue to want every moment of happiness to exist in your life. They will help you in any way they can, and fully respect your life's work. Enjoy every bit of the happiness that you have brought into your life.

Reverse: You have put in the work that has been necessary to bring all the components together to have bliss evolve into what is now present. However, it is not necessarily your bliss, but that of another's. You are part of their story, and giving support to another has played a part in growing your own happiness.

About the Image: As my Uber went careening through the streets of Lisbon, I happened to capture this amazing remnant from the art nouveau time period that had been integrated into the wall of a building. The expression of the face, quiet and confident, immediately inspired me to use it on this card.

Ten of Cups

Together this family has found strength. They are unified in their support, protection, and love. The Ten of Cups serves to remind us to rejoice in the power of connections, be it through family, chosen family, or friends. Being together through times of hardship and times of bliss is a part of every relationship. Be there, be present.

You are dearly loved and celebrated in another's life. It is not always necessary to be going and be active as a way to prove value, but rather in those quiet times with arms holding you close. When the world is not watching, we are soundly reminded that we are cherished by the kindred souls whom we share our lives with.

Reverse: It is easy to get lost in the Cups of emotions of what was. Although the moment may be over, the warm memories remain for a lifetime. It is best to appreciate that you were given the experience, and to allow it to flow like water, back to the universe and past.

About the Image: This card features a family of statues in a warm embrace located at the Jardim São Bento.

Page of Cups

With eyes of innocence and wonder, this youth takes in everything that exists in their world with a sense of awe. This curiosity to explore the world invokes a new and fresh perspective of the environment and emotional circumstances, with messages seeming to come from bizarre places at times. Be mindful to listen to them.

You are able to take a step back from the current situation and are seeing it through fresh eyes. What was once black and white is now fluid, with many variables coming into play that you are able to play out through pros and cons. You may have a quiet pop of an idea that floods your mind: write it down and reflect upon the words/action as they relate to what is at the forefront of your mind. It may be just the answer you were looking for.

Reverse: You are currently in the role of muse and messenger for another. This is a distinct shift, since what you say has power and influence in their forthcoming actions. Heed the responsibility with grace and humbleness.

About the Image: This Page sat just outside the Santa Casa da Misericórdia, in a small plaza.

Knight of Cups

Even before this Knight enters the scene, there is an energy that people can feel that is ready to appear at any time. Charismatic and charming, the draw to this person is nearly tangible, since everyone wants to be a part of their world. When in their presence, they make one feel as though they are the only one that matters, that they are loved and valued.

Should this energy be someone coming into your life, be prepared to be utterly smitten by the sheer confidence and joy they bring. There is a sense that absolutely nothing can go wrong; everything is ready to be dove into and grown. If you find that this is you, you may have a sense of or burst of energy that anything can be accomplished and that everyone is going to be right there to help you along the way. And you would be correct.

Reverse: The moment when things stagnate and boredom sets in is a dangerous time with this energy, since it wants to have things always flowing. Be ready, since this energy calls one to create change even when none is necessary for the situation, and may cause chaos.

About the Image: This card was inspired by the monument of King José I.

Queen of Cups

Sitting upon her book of knowledge, the Queen is lost in the realm of her own mind. Contemplating and reflecting, developing her psychic and intuitive abilities, are her hallmarks. She is sensitive to the needs of others, and while she may seem preoccupied in her thoughts, she is aware and reflective to ensure that her words and actions are supportive to those in her charge.

As this energy, or person, comes into your life, know that they may seem to know things before you even have to say anything. This can be unnerving, yet comforting, knowing that there is no need to repeat and recount your entire history to what brought you to here. She already knows and will be the supportive voice that brings comfort.

Reverse: You may be lost in a world within your mind. It is best to simply give yourself the time to be in deep thought to allow the messages from your subconscious to move forward. Be sure to let others know what is going on, since to be pulled back to the present can be jarring, and you may not be at your best to make immediate decisions or conversation.

About the image: This card was inspired by one of the statues in front of the Assembly of the Republic and is the building to the right of the figure in the background.

King of Cups

This King is a master over his emotions. There is very little that will unsettle him, since he knows to view the actions of others as simply their actions. He refrains from allowing others to emotionally manipulate him. This is due to him being able to detach himself from the emotional outcome of the situation, which tends to make him appear to be aloof.

When you have this energy come into your life as yourself or another, it is a sign that you/they truly are in control of your feelings and emotions, which makes it a perfect time to negotiate for what you want in your life to materialize. You are no longer being held captive emotionally to the outcome, so stay or go; it does not alter who you are intrinsically.

Reverse: You have gotten caught up in the emotional turmoil of those around you. They look to you as one who can solve their problems, but the reality is that you have enough happening in your own life. Time to step back and let them figure this out on their own.

About the Image: This King card was inspired by the statue that stands in the small plaza outside the Santa Casa da Misericórdia.

Suit of Pentacles

The suit of Pentacles is grounded in the world of abundance, wealth, and prosperity. This suit is conscious of the work it takes to bring financial gain to one's life. There is simply no easy-money method in this suit. It is going to take time, effort, and delayed gratification to see goals come to fruition. It is a suit that requires one to be prepared that any project begun when in this realm is slow to come to realization.

It is prudent to acknowledge that while at the core of this suit, it is about creating financial stability and growth, abundance and wealth are not always money related. One may be gifted with an abundance or a wealth of ideas, love, affection, or friends in their life.

When this suit comes up in readings, reflect upon the question before assuming that it is money related. A question that is focused on finding a romantic relationship that has a Four of Pentacles drawn may indicate that holding on to past experiences, accomplishments, or expectations may be preventing a new relationship from forming.

Ace of Pentacles

The Ace of Pentacles focuses on new beginnings in the realm of the material. There is an abundance and wealth of opportunities that are just through the arch. The only requirement is to take the steps necessary to put oneself onto the path for success.

You have made it to the gateway at the borders of where you have found stability and comfort. It can be terrifying as you step into a new realm, a new mindset, since you never know what the end results are going to be; do it anyway. Take the risk; give yourself the chance to have happiness, abundance, and prosperity through work and perseverance. You have the necessary skills, passion, and voice to bring it all together.

Reverse: As much as you are ready to escape through the archway into a new direction, it is an ungrounded aspiration and ill advised. There will be other opportunities, but right now you still need to bring past concerns to closure before moving ahead.

About the Image: This card is looking from inside the Arco da Rua Augusta toward the Praça do Comércio, which leads to the Tagus River, which can take one to all points beyond.

Two of Pentacles

The Two of Pentacles brings into the conversation the idea of management. His lackadaisical pose underlines his need to manage time, resources, relationships, and so on to bring balance into his life. Balance is achieved not by giving energy and attention equally, but by recognizing that which requires greater work receives what it needs to keep it manageable and keep the momentum going. The minor concerns will continue to move forward just fine with being checked in upon from time to time.

As you learn and develop better self-management, what once controlled you and your life you have now taken back underfoot. You are firmly in place to control how the narrative plays out, by prioritizing aspects of your life and the energy you are willing to commit to each. This comes from a place of strength and self-awareness. As this grows, it will transfer into other areas of your life, improving and smoothing over what was once rough waters.

Reverse: You are fully at the mercy of the demands others have been placing upon your time and resources. It is going to take hard work to shift the energy, since each wave brings a new layer onto the situation, and it may feel as though you are only able to keep your head above water.

About the Image: This card was inspired by the lounging figure on the left side of the Arco da Rua Augusta.

Three of Pentacles

The architect approached the trader craftsman to discuss and share methods of improving the dilapidated, uninhabitable building to bring it back to usefulness. Each was respectful of the expertise and knowledge that they brought to the meeting. They were ready to assemble the necessary people and finances to bring the project to fruition.

It is through collaboration that you are able to see projects move from the starting ground and into completion. This is a positive development since it signifies that the people you need to help you with your ideas are going to be there, or that you will be called upon due to your expertise in the field.

Reverse: Be careful whom you welcome onto a project. Check references and reviews and strive to find former people who have worked with or contracted this business or person. They may not be representing themselves honestly. Be sure that you are presenting yourself in an honest light for any new opportunity or need as well.

About the image: This card came together in a collaboration of sights in Lisbon. The building in the background was in utter disrepair. Lisbon has an active group of investors repairing and bringing these buildings back. The man on the right in the brown is St. Joseph, located at the Basilica da Estrela, and the man in the green is one of the lead poets from the sixteenth century on display at the Praça Luís de Camões.

Four of Pentacles

The woman stood upon what she firmly mastered while holding in each hand evidence of her accomplishments. Head raised high, she took pride in the results of her hard work. Each discus had a story engraved upon it of her journey, which she was unwilling to simply discard. Due to this, many often saw her as being controlling, greedy, and staying in the past.

You have worked hard to get to where you are now, and each experience is a testament to your resolve to attain your goals. Embrace each and then consider what are the next steps that you can use to move toward and continue your journey and growth. Staying in one spot without growth invites stagnation and can cause you to become irrelevant in your field.

Reverse: You once controlled your direction and accomplishments, but now your work is driven by the views of what others feel you should be doing to be seen as worthy. You continue to chase what their dreams are for you. Is it time to begin to pull back to live your own dreams again?

About the Image: This card was inspired by the figure that stands just to the left of the main doors to the Basílica da Estrela.

Five of Pentacles

The woman holds a mirror to reflect back upon herself, allowing herself to become enchanted by visual engagement. This action gave her reason to ignore her reality for a brief moment: the hardships that she was facing, including the help that stood right behind her.

When we are caught in a time of personal struggle, we become so engrossed in the moment that we often neglect to see that there is always help, be it counseling through emotional trauma, financial assistance, community programs, or the help of family and friends. We are taught not to complain and to persevere through our problems, but now is the time to reach out and let others know of your struggle. Get help before things move to crisis.

Reverse: At this point, you can no longer stay where you are; the situation has turned from bad to worse.

The time to leave is now. Make a plan with friends or family to help you get back on your feet immediately.

About the Image: This card was inspired by the Basilica da Estrela from the outside, and one of the statues that stands to watch over those who pass by and enter.

Six of Pentacles

The woman watched closely as the coinage was placed on the table, ensuring that it was to the agreed-on amount for the wares she held in her arms. Regardless of any hindrance, her work was still just as valued as another, and she had learned to advocate her worth.

As you are compensated for your work, be sure to stay aware of the current financial trends of others in your field. It is important for your expertise that you remain properly compensated, since people will view your pay as a sign of your worth. You are worth every cent, if not more.

Reverse: You find yourself in negotiations. You know what you are willing to pay, but it comes with a trade-off in quality. You will need to weigh out the pros and cons of what this costs and what you are willing to accept in return.

About the Image: This card was inspired by a statue that sits in the middle of a pond at the Jardim da Estrela. It caught me that even with the loss of a hand, she was featured as having bounty in her hands and a kind demeanor.

Seven of Pentacles

Much like the Ace of Pentacles, with the arch that leads to a world of manifesting opportunities, the Seven of Pentacles is much more focused on precisely what is desired and the willingness to take the journey to reach the goal. Distractions and other avenues of pursuit emerge along the way, but ultimately, knowing what resides on the other side of the doors is well worth leaving them behind.

You have made your way through the first arch from the Ace of Pentacles and learned to balance your needs and wants in the Two of Pentacles, and now your goal is within sight. Will there potentially be some unforeseen challenges? Most certainly, since none can control what may be off to the side at the end of the tunnel. But with a momentary pause for the perfect moment to cross and make it to the goal, it is worth the wait.

Reverse: Now that you have worked diligently to this point, take a breath and reflect on the repercussions of what will change once you open the door. Are you truly ready for this? If so, move forward with confidence. Should there be any hesitation, take the time you need to reflect on why you feel this.

About the Image: As I was walking past this location, I was enchanted by the effect of the warm yellow with the red door at the end. I wanted to break from my mission and lose myself in the world I saw just through the tunnel.

Eight of Pentacles

Commitment and due diligence to the mastery of craft and knowledge drove the man to continue his studies without distraction of the day-to-day encumbrances. While his focus was honorable, his drive left those around him to ponder if they mattered. From time to time, he needed to ensure that while he was working to better his situation, those closest to him remained an important aspect.

Your dedication to bettering your life is a tremendous step that needs to be honored, and the time commitment needed to be understood by everyone in your life. As you are working toward your goal, remain aware that the ones closest to you who connect emotionally may feel neglected. While they absolutely support your growth, they still desire to have time with you. It is advisable that while you are working, make sure to take time to connect and check in with those you love and support you.

Reverse: You are in a time of hyperfocus to gain the knowledge you need in order to move toward your goals needed to achieve your professional growth.

Be aware that during this time, your personal relationships may be affected adversely.

About the Image: This card was inspired by one of the pediment figures found at the Assembly of the Republic. Even from afar, I was struck by the meticulous nature.

Nine of Pentacles

The Nine of Pentacles tells one to take time to relax. There is no need to rush or worry, since this is a well-deserved moment of reprieve to reflect on the dedication it has taken to move to this space. Hard work and effort made this level of comfort and security happen, and should be enjoyed before stepping away and back to the rush of the real world.

The luxuries in life happen often in tandem with practiced fidelity toward one's goals. By envisioning what it is that you ultimately want, it enables you to establish a plan and understand that delayed gratification is necessary to have this dream come to fruition. It is absolutely possible, and should you already be at this point, congratulations on your hard work coming together.

Reverse: The current situation has caused your secure and protected life to begin to feel that it is more of a prison than a life of comfort. It is time to let go of the material entrapments, open the gate, and begin to live again.

About the Image: This card was inspired by a character found in the pediment at the Assembly of the Republic.

Ten of Pentacles

The Ten of Pentacles signifies the success of manifesting one's goals. The work and dedication that have gone into this moment have paid off in larger dividends than could have been realized at the beginning of the journey. From stepping through the arch and into a world of opportunity, the growth and abundance that one now is able to reflect upon were worth the adventure.

You are a living testament to the results of following your dreams to fruition. Reflecting upon the journey serves to remind you of how much you have changed to be prepared for this new role. Enjoy the abundance that fills your life in all aspects, and cherish the moment.

Reverse: Be sure to document and share your journey with others. This works to help educate others of the dedication you have put into the moment, and to acknowledge that what they see now did not just magically happen or that you got a lucky break. Everything that has come together was done with intention and work.

About the Image: The family featured in this card was found in the pediment of the Assembly of the Republic, signaling to me the Portuguese connection of protecting families. The background is of the many arches throughout the city.

Page of Pentacles

The Page of Pentacles holds in his hand the beginnings of a new opportunity to grow one's wealth and abundance. This may be in the form of new skills and knowledge that help get a promotion at work, or a new job that pays a higher wage. This is a fresh energy that opens doors, and one just needs to walk on into the adventure.

You have been given a gift in your hands of a golden opportunity. Be sure to utilize this to the very best means possible to help it manifest into the abundance that you desire. An opportunity would not be presented to you if others felt that you were not up to the task to see it through to completion. They know of your dedication and diligent nature. You truly are the right person.

Reverse: You may be handed an opportunity that simply does not feel right, and chances are it isn't. The other parties have not been clear as to the work or parameters needed to be done that would facilitate you to receive compensation. This also may seem a bit too easy. If it is, something is not right, and it would be best to let go and move on.

About the Image: This Page card was inspired by one of the figures that watches over those who approach the Basilica da Estrela. The greenery is from a collection of trees at the Jardim da Estela, which sits across the street from the church.

Knight of Pentacles

This Knight stands just outside the city's archway, taking a moment before committing himself to his task at hand. He knows that things take time to come to fruition, and patience in the matter is what will make all the difference in his success in a venture.

When this energy comes along in your life, be prepared that what you have started, you will need to finish regardless of the time it takes. You must be actively involved in all aspects and refrain from thinking that someone else will do the job for you. This is squarely on your shoulders if it is to succeed.

Reverse: You will need to let go of this project. There are concerns that you have brought up that have not been succinctly clarified for you to be able to see it through successfully. Be sure to stand your ground on your expectations and be willing to walk away.

About the Image: This card was inspired by the monument to King José I that sits before the Arco da Rua Augusta.

Queen of Pentacles

The Queen of Pentacles sits with her wealth plainly out for all to see. She is responsible for her financial independence and successes, which she openly shares, and she welcomes everyone to her realm. She is gracious and kind with a desire to help everyone succeed and find their happiness in any way that she can.

This Queen may represent you or someone in your life. Warm and generous to those who are loved, she ensures that everyone knows how she values having them around her. She works to keep them safe and free from ever experiencing scarcity. If this is you, then you are loved as deeply as you love others in your world.

Reverse: You are seen as the foundation of the family, keeping everyone connected. Should anyone of those you love fall onto hard times, you are right there to help them get back on their feet, without hesitation. The current situation may require that you reach out and reiterate this to your loved ones or ask for the help you may need.

About the Image: **This Queen can be found at the Jardim Dom Luís, beside the Mercado da Ribeira.**

King of Pentacles

The King of Pentacles was born with the innate nature of bringing and growing abundance in his life. He works diligently to pull together the right people to ensure success for any project he launches. To look in from the outside, it would appear that anything he touches suddenly turns into a great success story. He is a humble man and would never allow another to know the long hours he puts in to find a way to bring whatever is before him to success.

To have a person of this nature in your life, or if it represents you, is truly a gift of fortuitous circumstance. The perseverance and dedication to seeing a project through to the end with creative means for success creates a calling card of sorts.

People may begin to seek you in order to help them bring their ideas to prosperity, which will help you generate additional revenue as a consultant.

Reverse: You have projects in mind that will truly help the world and bring in additional wealth to you. The choice in how you move forward and what projects you take on is ultimately yours. Be mindful to not overwhelm yourself with so many projects that you forget to live and connect with others that matter most in your life.

About the Image: This King was found just to the right of the Assembly of the Republic. Jose Estevao Coelho De Magalhaes was a noted political speaker from the 19th century.

Spreads

Sails Away

There is an element of adventure and exploration that runs through the veins of Lisboa. Do you go this way? Or do you go that way? This spread is intended as a reflection on the pros and cons of a choice to help make a sound decision.

Begin by shuffling the cards while considering the topic that you are debating upon in your mind.

Pull from the pile as you deem the best and what you are comfortable with, be it from the top, middle, or bottom. Arrange the cards as shown on p. 121. As you flip over the cards, each one is coordinated to answer the following questions:

Card 1: Main Signifier card: How is this situation affecting me?

Card 2: What is my first option to resolve the situation?

Card 3: What is my second option to resolve the situation?

Card 4: What is the outcome of using this option?

Card 5: What is the outcome of using this option?

At this point, the choice is truly up to you in how you utilize this reflection of the ways that help bring a decision to the matters that weigh on your mind.

Bridge to a New Life

This spread helps give perspective to some of the work that will need to take place for those who would like to map out a plan to move from one point in their life to the next. It also reflects on how this change will change them intrinsically.

Start by shuffling the cards while envisioning what you are wanting to achieve: picture the colors of the space, the sounds, the feel of being in that place. Once you have a solid picture in your mind's eye, ask, "How do I make this come to fruition / make this happen?"

Pull from the pile as you deem the best and what you are comfortable with, be it from the top, middle, or bottom. Then arrange the cards according to the images shown on p. 123. As you flip over the cards, each one is coordinated to answer the following questions:

> Card 1: What is the first skill I need to develop to help me achieve my plan?

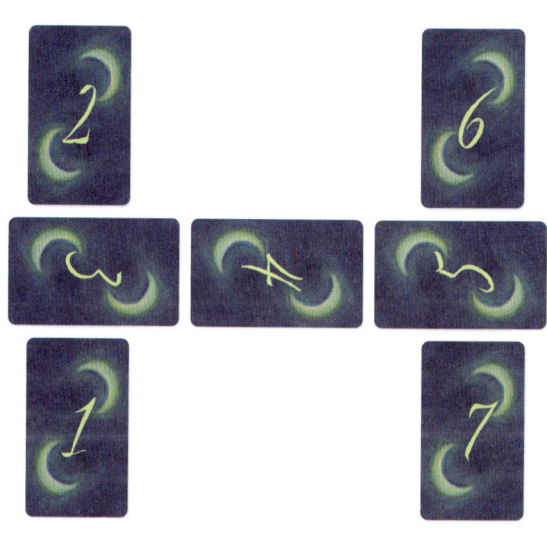

Card 2: What is the second skill I need to develop to help me achieve my plan?

Card 3: What is the third skill I need to develop to help me achieve my plan?

Card 4: What challenging situation will develop?

Card 5: How can I ensure the best approach to resolve the situation?

Card 6: How will these changes affect those around me?

Card 7: How does this experience change me?

Conclusion

I hope that you have enjoyed the adventures and art of the *Lisboa Tarot*. May you have the blessings to visit this remarkable place!

About Beth Seilonen

Beth first began working and studying Tarot while taking a class on understanding semiotics in art during her college years. She was intrigued by how we placed meaning between the symbols to a life experience. This led her to be more reflective of how these symbols were relevant in our current world and how it could be improved on.

Beth continued to explore this concept and how the shift in character perspective will shift the narrative intention. Drawing upon humor and reflective insight, her decks challenge one to strive to grow into the best versions of themselves.

She has currently created more than 100 decks, including the Major Arcana, Tarot, Lenormand, and Oracles. Her mass-produced works currently include *Tarot Leaves*, *Bleu Cat Tarot*, *Dream Raven Tarot*, *Guardian Tarot*, *Ravyness Drakon Tarot*, and the upcoming deck *Flowering Souls Oracle*, as well as *Tarot at the Crossroads* (written by Shannon MacLeod), all available through Schiffer Publishing / REDFeather.

Beth's limited-edition decks and artwork can be found by visiting www.bethseilonen.com.

Copyright © 2023 by Beth Seilonen
Library of Congress Control Number: 2023931149

All rights reserved. No part of this work may be reproduced or used in any form or by any means—graphic, electronic, or mechanical, including photocopying or information storage and retrieval systems—without written permission from the publisher.

The scanning, uploading, and distribution of this book or any part thereof via the Internet or any other means without the permission of the publisher is illegal and punishable by law. Please purchase only authorized editions and do not participate in or encourage the electronic piracy of copyrighted materials.

"Red Feather Mind Body Spirit" logo is a trademark of Schiffer Publishing, Ltd.
"Red Feather Mind Body Spirit Feather" logo is a registered trademark of Schiffer Publishing, Ltd.

Designed by Danielle D. Farmer
Type set in Dream Big/Poppins

ISBN: 978-0-7643-6698-7
Printed in China

Published by REDFeather Mind, Body, Spirit
An imprint of Schiffer Publishing, Ltd.
4880 Lower Valley Road
Atglen, PA 19310
Phone: (610) 593-1777; Fax: (610) 593-2002
Email: info@redfeathermbs.com
Web: www.redfeathermbs.com

Beth Seilonen

Lisboa Tarot

Tarot through the Streets of Lisbon

REDFeather™
MIND | BODY | SPIRIT

4880 Lower Valley Road, Atglen, PA 19310